# LIFE
## ATTITUDES

# LIFE
## ATTITUDES

A 5-session course on
the Beatitudes

ROBERT WARREN AND SUE MAYFIELD

Church House Publishing
Church House
Great Smith Street
London SW1P 3AZ

ISBN 978 0 7151 4233 2

First published by
Church House Publishing in 2004.
Third Impression 2013

Typeset by
Church House Publishing

Printed and bound by Halstan, Amersham.

# >> Contents

# Matthew 5.3-10

Blessed are the poor in spirit, for theirs is the kingdom of heaven.

Blessed are those who mourn, for they will be comforted.

Blessed are the meek, for they will inherit the earth.

Blessed are those who hunger and thirst for righteousness,

> for they will be filled.

Blessed are the merciful, for they will receive mercy.

Blessed are the pure in heart, for they will see God.

Blessed are the peacemakers, for they will be called children of God.

Blessed are those who are persecuted for righteousness' sake,

> for theirs is the kingdom of heaven.

# >> Introduction

The aim of this course is to explore and grapple with the Beatitudes –
or beautiful attitudes – described by Jesus in the Sermon on the Mount.
These eight radical sayings from Matthew's Gospel (Matthew 5.3-10)
contain both values for living and promises of blessing.

Christianity is essentially a 'lifestyle' religion. It is as much about what
and who we are as about what we say or believe. The Scriptures are not
primarily books of doctrine, but rather stories of how the revelation of
God has made an impact on and shaped the lives of those who have
heard its message.

We live in a rapidly changing world. Increasingly, ours is a culture where
people are less interested in religious activity than in 'spirituality', and
more interested in 'resources for living' than in doctrines or creeds. In
a climate where lifestyle and well-being are major preoccupations and
where values and codes are judged by whether they *work*, the challenge
for the Church is twofold: to equip its members more wholly to *live* their
faith; and to demonstrate to those outside the Church that a knowledge
of God makes sense of the whole of life. The Beatitudes focus our
minds on what makes us truly happy. These eight short verses are
a rich mine of resources for living. They call us to 'live the kingdom –
now' and to encounter God's blessing as we do this.

Throughout history, Christians have seen the Beatitudes as a key part
of Jesus' teaching. In them Jesus encapsulated the key characteristics
of those who seek to embrace his kingdom. Moreover, Jesus modelled
the Beatitudes himself in his earthly life. The sayings are both the
template by which he lived and the definition of what it means to follow
him. In describing the characteristics of those who will inherit and
inhabit the kingdom of God (both now and in eternity) the Beatitudes
describe the 'likeness of Christ'.

These words offer us a self-portrait of Jesus . . . The whole message of the Gospel is this: Become like Jesus. We have his self-portrait. When we keep that in front of our eyes, we will soon learn what it means to follow Jesus and become like him.

*Henri Nouwen*, Bread for the Journey, *p.163*

. . . the more I study Jesus, the more I realize that the statements contained here lie at the heart of his message. If I fail to understand this teaching, I fail to understand him.

*Philip Yancey*, The Jesus I Never Knew, *p.103*

# >> Why do this course during Lent?

Lent is traditionally a season when Christians re-examine their spiritual lives and review what it means to be a follower of Christ. In the Early Church, Lent was a time of preparation for those who were to be baptized at Easter. In past centuries, the Beatitudes have played a vital role in the initiation of newcomers to the faith.

Studying the Beatitudes will undoubtedly deepen our understanding of Jesus and challenge our deepest personal values. However, we cannot and should not limit the Beatitudes to our inner devotional lives. They touch the whole of life. They speak to our relationships with those who are closest to us, and to our work context (or lack of it). They also address the culture, values and political structures of the country in which we live. They impact on our attitude to, and connection with, major global issues such as environmental pollution and the deep-seated hostilities and injustices that afflict our world. Studying the Beatitudes during this season offers all Christians an opportunity to reflect on their discipleship, both individual and corporate.

If we take the Beatitudes seriously, their effects will be costly and life-changing. Jesus' 'beautiful attitudes' in many ways cut across the values of our times. To live 'Beatitudinally' is to live 'counterculturally' in ways that will often set us at odds with the world around us.

The writer Philip Yancey asks:

---

What meaning can the Beatitudes have for a society that honours the self-assertive, confident and rich? Blessed are the happy and strong, we believe. Blessed are those who hunger and thirst for a good time, who look out for Number One.

*Philip Yancey, The Jesus I Never Knew, p.106*

---

The aim of this course is to explore answers to that question, for ourselves, our churches and our society.

It is our hope and prayer that those who follow the course will be sent out from it with a stronger sense of:
> **Encountering** the person of Christ.
> **Choosing** to live God's way.
> **Embracing** the cost of following Christ.
> **Experiencing** the blessing God has promised those who live as children of the kingdom.

## >>What does the course consist of?

The course consists of 5 sessions each designed to last about 90 minutes.
> **Session 1** looks at the Beatitudes as a whole and invites the group to take an overview of the eight sayings.
> **Sessions 2–5** take an in-depth look at the sayings, focusing on two of the Beatitudes in each session.
> **Session 5** allows time for summary and reflection on the whole course.

Each session contains study guidelines, interactive activities and ideas for prayer and meditation. (See pp. 7–10 for a fuller description of the features of each session.) There are also ideas for practical action and suggestions for further study.

## >>Who is the course for?

The course is designed for group study and many of the activities involve sharing together. An ideal size for the group would be between eight and twelve people.

We suggest that in Sessions 2, 3, 4 and 5 you divide the group into two for part of the session so that each smaller group can look closely at one of the pair of Beatitudes and then feed back their responses to the whole group. Smaller groups may find this difficult, in which case we suggest you miss out some of the material, focusing on just one of the Beatitudes during the study time and the other in the closing meditation.

To get the most from the course, we suggest that each group member has a copy of the book.

## >>Where should we meet?

The best meeting place for a course of this kind is probably someone's home. Alternatively you could meet in a church hall or other community venue. Wherever you meet, make sure the venue is welcoming, comfortable, warm and easy for everyone to get to. If you are splitting into two groups, it is good, where possible, to have these groups in separate rooms: two groups in the same room tend to distract each other.

You may like to provide refreshments before or after the session, in which case be aware that you will need to add on extra time to the recommended 90-minute session.

## >>Who can lead the course?

This material has been designed so that most people, with a little preparation and thought, could lead it. You do not need to be a 'theological expert' or experienced in adult education (although experience does, of course, help).

The leader's main task is not to teach or lecture the group, but to facilitate discussion and exploration by group members by leading them through the material provided.

As well as preparing and handling the study material and ensuring that prayer and meditation times go well, the leader should be aware of the dynamics of the group and alive to the joys and struggles of each group member.

Leading a group study can be an onerous task if attempted by one person alone so you might like to consider sharing the leadership with someone else.

Remember that growth in the Christian life is not just about accumulating knowledge. There are things to learn here, but, more importantly, group members will be encouraged to reflect upon and to share their own experiences of life and of their learning during the course.

*If you are planning to lead the* Life Attitudes *course you might find the following* Tips for leaders *helpful.*

For more tips on running a study group, see the booklet *Leading an Emmaus Group* (CHP, second edition, 2004).

# >>Tips for leaders

## Be prepared

Make sure that you are familiar with the content of each session. You will need to decide beforehand which parts of the material you are going to use and whether you are going to split into smaller groups for some of the activities.

For each session we have provided background information to help with understanding each of the Beatitudes and the passage as a whole. Make sure you read this information thoroughly. It is there to help you. It is *not* designed to be used verbatim in the session. The aim of each session is to help group members towards a discovery of the meaning of each Beatitude for themselves rather than to tell them what to think.

If you are doing the 'Input' part of the *Encounter* section prepare what you will say in advance. Try not to say too much or to waffle. Make a few points clearly and well. You might like to practise what you will say so that when it comes to it you won't have to have your nose in your notes!

## Delegate

Don't do everything yourself. Share out tasks with co-leaders or other group members. Not only does this help the leader, but it also gives others the chance to exercise and develop their own gifts of leading and contributing to the group. You might ask someone to read the Bible passage or to lead an opening prayer or the closing meditation. You might delegate the role of welcoming people or making the refreshments. You could invite someone else to be a group 'facilitator', if you decide to split into smaller groups.

*Make sure you give people plenty of warning* and don't land them with difficult tasks at the last minute. Be there to offer support and advice if needed. If you designate someone as a group facilitator give that person the opportunity to look at the material beforehand.

## Be organized!

> Try to arrive at the venue in good time so that you aren't doing last-minute preparations as people are arriving.

> Set the room up carefully, arranging the furniture so that there is a good group dynamic, with no one left out and everybody able to see the leader (and flipchart or video/DVD if you are using one).

> Make sure that you have pens, pencils, large sheets of paper, and any craft materials, music or objects ready beforehand. There is a checklist at the beginning of each session telling you what you will need.

> Make sure, if you are reading the printed prayers together or saying them responsorially, that group members have copies.

## Be imaginative

We all know that people learn in different ways: some people like to take in information by reading and reflection in quiet, others learn best through group discussion, others like to respond to visual stimuli (e.g., a piece of art or a centrepiece used as a focal point in worship). Others like to respond through art and craft or through music.

The course provides you with a range of teaching methods and ideas. Suggestions are made – especially in the *Go deep* . . . sections – for creative, multimedia responses to the Beatitudes. We encourage you to be inventive and to draw on your own and the group's creativity, as appropriate.

## Be flexible

We have provided enough material for a session of about 90 minutes. Allow extra time for refreshments before or afterwards if you wish.

The suggested timings are guides. But remember that it is better to do too little and leave people wanting more rather than try and cover too much and leave people exhausted. If you are going to go over the agreed time, warn people – and try not to make a habit of it.

## >>How each session works

Material for the course is in two sections for each of the five sessions: *Beforehand* and *The Session*.

*Beforehand* contains:

> **Aims of the session** – to help focus your mind in preparation and evaluate sessions after the event;

> **What you will need** – a checklist of practical materials required to ensure smooth running of the session (see pp. 11–12 for a more comprehensive list of resources);

> **Background to the Bible material** – to help you understand the Beatitudes and their context. Some groups might like to read this material for themselves in advance of the sessions. Alternatively it can be read by the leader or leaders and then summarized in the 'Input' section. The *Background* material for Session 1 gives a general overview of the Beatitudes as a whole. *Background* material for Sessions 2–5 provides information and insights for each Beatitude under four headings.

1 **Diamond truth** – an attempt to summarize the essence of the Beatitude, taking as inspiration 'The truth is like a multi-faceted diamond – too brilliant, too exquisite, to be fully illuminated by a single source of light' (Walter Wink, *Transforming Bible Study*, p. 37).

2 **Consequences** – some ideas about the practical, real-life implications of taking the truth of the Beatitude to heart and living it out.

3 **Cutting across** – identifying ways in which this saying of Jesus 'cuts across' the values of our society (and/or church!) and is countercultural.

4 **Missing the point** – a round-up of common misconceptions or misreadings of each of the Beatitudes.

*The Session* is structured under the following headings:

 Welcome

 Action replay

 Brainstorm

 Encounter

 Talk about it

 Get real!

 Go deep . . .

Each session follows the same structure. The sections of the course work in the following ways (please note that timings are only approximate suggestions):

## >>Welcome (5–10 minutes)

The leader welcomes the group and puts them at their ease. This is particularly important in the first session, especially if yours is a new group meeting for the first time. The notes for Session 1 give some suggestions of how to help a new group to gel.

Someone leads the group in prayer and/or the group say the Course Prayer together. The purpose of this opening prayer is to still people from the busy-ness of the day and the rush of getting to the meeting, and to turn their thoughts to God. Each group will have its own preferences as to how it prays. If the group is well established, it may already have developed a pattern for prayer. Suggestions are given in the session notes but feel free to use whatever is most appropriate for your group.

**Remember:** If you ask another member of the group to lead this part of the session, make sure they have plenty of time for preparation, and guidance if needed. Ensure that no one does it under duress or feels 'dropped in it'.

## >>Action replay (10 minutes)

An opportunity for group members to report on what they noticed, thought about or did in response to the previous session's *Get real!* section.

## >>Brainstorm (5 minutes)

A quick ice-breaker to be done individually, in pairs or as a whole group.

## >>Encounter [15 minutes]

The group encounter the Beatitudes by:

> **Reading** the Bible passage.

> **Input** – a short talk from the leader based on his or her reading of the *Background*. This may be cut or omitted altogether if group members prefer to read the *Background* for themselves before the session.

## >>Talk about it [25–30 minutes]

This is the main group study activity consisting of questions for discussion and a Jesus focus, which links the Beatitude(s) being studied with incidents from Jesus' life. Depending on numbers, you may wish to do this as a whole group or to split into two smaller groups and then report back to each other.

## >>Get real! [10 minutes]

Each week suggestions will be made for ways in which the group can put into practice the insights and values that have been discussed during the session. Projects may be individual tasks or whole-group activities.

## >>Go deep . . . [15 minutes]

This section offers an extended meditation to close the session. A number of suggestions are given to enable you to choose something appropriate to your group. Make sure this part is not omitted or rushed. This is a vital time to help the group to:

> slow down and reflect in silence on what has been the dominant theme for them and on what they feel has spoken to them through the session;

> grasp the meaning of the Beatitude at a deep personal level;

> identify its application to their lives and to the wider community.

# >>Resources

## Music

We have suggested that you use music to prepare for prayer and during the *Go deep . . .* sections. The following recommendations might be useful:

> **Taizé** several CDs are available, including *Wait for the Lord* (Gia, 1995) and *Taizé Chant* (Decca, 2006) available on CD and as MP3 downloads from Amazon.co.uk and elsewhere;

> **Instrumental Praise** Series of CDs and MP3 downloads (Brentwood, 1999);

> *Smooth Classics: The Ultimate Collection* (Classic FM, 2008);

## Musical settings of the Beatitudes

> **Arvo Pärt**, *Berliner Messe* (Naxos, 2004, track 11) available on CD and as an MP3 download;

> *The Liturgy of St John Chrysostom*, performed by the Russian Orthodox Cathedral Choir (Ikon, 2000),

> **Sweet Honey In The Rock**, *Selections 1970–1988* (Flying Fish Records, 1997);

> **Taizé**, *Bless the Lord* (Pilgrim, track 9) CD and MP3 download.

## Objects

You might like to place objects on a low table or on the floor as a visual focus during the *Welcome* or *Go deep . . .* sections. Suitable objects might be:

> flowers or a plant;

> pebbles or stones;

> a candle;

> twigs or driftwood;

> a cross or crucifix;

> a Bible;

> a carving or figure, e.g. of people praying or embracing.

## Images

If you want to use images of Christ as a visual focus try:

> **The Christ We Share**, Picture Resource Collection from CMS/USPG.

> **Icon postcards** – many cathedrals, churches or religious bookshops sell postcard images. Alternatively try using www.google.co.uk. Click on 'Images' and then type in 'religious icons'.

Please see also the *Bibliography and Further Resources* at the back of the book.

# >> 1 Living Well/Beforehand

## Introducing the Beatitudes (Matthew 5.3-10)

## >>Aim

This session aims to introduce the Beatitudes, giving an overview of all eight sayings as a prelude to the rest of the course.

### What you will need

> - flipchart and marker pens;
> - A4 paper and pens;
> - copies of this book (preferably one each);
> - candle, objects or images of Christ
>   (optional – see pp. 11–12).

## >>Background

### What are 'Beatitudes'?

The sayings of Jesus that we call the Beatitudes (Matthew 5.3-10) come at the beginning of the three chapters in Matthew's Gospel (Chapters 5–7) that are referred to as the Sermon on the Mount. There is another version of the sayings in Luke 6.17-19.

The *Oxford English Dictionary* gives the meaning of the word 'Beatitude' as '1. Supreme blessedness or happiness. 2. An ascription of special blessedness, especially those pronounced by Christ in the Sermon on the Mount.'

Most versions of the Bible use the word 'Blessed', although some versions, such as the Good News, translate the word as 'Happy'.

For some, the word 'Blessed' has become so overfamiliar and wellworn that Jesus' words lose their impact. As Philip Yancey puts it: 'Blessed is far too sedate . . . to carry the percussive force Jesus intended. The Greek word conveys something like a short cry of joy, "Oh you lucky person!"' (*The Jesus I Never Knew*, p. 105).

## Unlocking the Beatitudes

The Beatitudes are a closed book to many of us. We struggle to understand them and when we glimpse their meaning we aren't sure if we agree with them! To some they appear to be a 'charter for wimps'. They can seem to be so other-worldly and unattainable – impossible to practise in real life.

Throughout history, the Beatitudes have suffered serious misinterpretation. Church, history, and society itself, have often distorted their meaning. Sometimes they have been confined to a purely personal, privatized spirituality when – though certainly life-changing for the individual believer – they embrace communal, global and political agendas too. Some people have suggested that the Beatitudes simply reflect different personality types; with the shrinking violets practising meekness and the aggressive ones among us being those who suffer persecution.

So how can we know what Jesus meant by the Beatitudes? There is a simple answer. The Beatitudes are about the characteristics of the children of the kingdom, children of the heavenly Father. And the supreme role model for such a calling is Jesus Christ himself.

How Jesus lived is the key to the interpretation of the Beatitudes. He is the living embodiment of these truths. His whole life is therefore a commentary on them.

# The shape of the Beatitudes

There is a wonderful beauty, order and rhythm in the eight Beatitudes.

> Each one begins with the assurance of God's blessing.

> Each one describes a kingdom characteristic or value,
  which Jesus says is foundational to living as a child of the
  heavenly Father.

> Each one ends with a promise of what lies ahead for those
  on this particular path.

All the promises refer to blessings – some of which are promised in
the future and some of which are promised now. This balance of 'now'
and 'not yet' expresses the paradox in the teaching of Jesus that the
kingdom has come among us, yet we are to pray for its coming.

A further symmetry is that the fourth and eighth Beatitudes are both
about *righteousness*. One is about hungering for it, the other about
suffering persecution because of it. Maturity in God's sight is about
eagerly seeking after righteousness but also being willing to suffer for
it. This suggests that the interpretation of the Beatitudes as a 'charter
for wimps' cannot stand. Working and fighting for righteousness do not
fit with a weak approach to life – things certainly did not work out like
that in the life of Jesus.

# The significance of the Beatitudes

In some ways, the Beatitudes are to the New Testament what the Ten
Commandments are to the Old Testament. Both outline a lifestyle
desirable to God. The Beatitudes, however, are not laws – rather they
are statements of grace. They overflow with affirmation, accepting love
and reassurance. Blessing, gift, hope, encouragement, grace; these are
the foundations on which the kingdom announced by Jesus is built. This
speaks to the depths of who we are, for so often we are actually more
at home 'trying hard to be good', than we are in receiving the goodness
and gift of God's love. The Beatitudes take us into a whole new realm of
living by and in the grace of God.

## >>Welcome (10 minutes)

### Introductions

Make sure members of the group know each other's names and are made to feel welcome. If this is a new group meeting for the first time, invite members of the group to introduce themselves. You could divide everyone into pairs, give the pairs five minutes to introduce themselves to each other, then ask each person to introduce their partner to the rest of the group.

### Pray

Create a still atmosphere. You might like to light a candle, play some music or encourage people to focus on a visual resource such as a cross or image of Christ (see suggestions on pp. 11–12).

Either pray in your own words, asking God to help you as you begin your course of study, or use the Course Prayer. One person could read it out or you could say it corporately.

#### Course Prayer

Almighty God
Thank you that you meet us where we are
And beckon us into your kingdom.
As we journey together
May we encounter Christ Jesus,
Be empowered to live like him,
And understand more fully what it means to be blessed. Amen.

## >>Brainstorm (5 minutes)

Ask the group: *What makes you happy?*
Do this in whatever way suits the temperament of your group.

Here are some suggestions:
> Ask people to shout out answers and write them on
  a flipchart.
> Ask people to compile lists together in twos or threes and
  then read them out.
> Ask people to write one idea on a piece of paper and put it in
  a basket then give the scraps of paper out again so everyone
  reads out someone else's contribution.

Try to give spontaneous answers and don't challenge or mock each
other's suggestions.

## >>Encounter [35 minutes]

### Read the Beatitudes [Matthew 5.3-10]

Ask a member of the group to read Matthew 5.3-10 (give them some
warning so they can prepare in advance). Alternatively, read it aloud
together. (You might want to decide in advance whether you are going
to say 'Blessed' or 'Bless-ed'.) Another approach is to play one of the
musical settings listed on p. 11.

---

Blessed are the poor in spirit, for theirs is
    the kingdom of heaven.
Blessed are those who mourn, for they will be comforted.
Blessed are the meek, for they will inherit the earth.
Blessed are those who hunger and thirst for righteousness,
    for they will be filled.
Blessed are the merciful, for they will receive mercy.
Blessed are the pure in heart, for they will see God.
Blessed are the peacemakers, for they will be called
    children of God.
Blessed are those who are persecuted for righteousness' sake,
    for theirs is the kingdom of heaven.

*Matthew 5.3-10*

---

Allow a period of silence to follow so that the words can sink in. After the silence, read the passage again and ask the group to think about the following questions (write them on a flipchart in advance if you have one):

> What strikes you most? (**!**)

> What puzzles you most? (**?**)

> What gives you most hope? (**✔**)

> What do the Beatitudes leave you wanting to discover or do?(**>>**)

Now feed back your impressions as a group. You could do this in the following way:

1 In the middle of a flipchart draw an oval and write the word 'Beatitudes' fairly small, to the top of the oval.

2 In the four corners of the sheet draw the four symbols shown in brackets after the above questions and write group members' responses to each of the questions underneath the symbols.

## Input

Now using the *Background* information on pp. 13–15 give a brief introduction to the Beatitudes. You might wish to include the following:

> a definition of the word 'Beatitude';

> an acknowledgement that these verses of Scripture are difficult – both to understand and to practise;

> a reassurance that the passage invites us to live by grace;

> a brief description of the shape of the eight sayings.

## >>Talk about it (15 minutes)

Break into smaller groups of two or more (depending on your numbers) and give each group a large sheet of paper and a marker pen. Invite the groups to write a slogan or shoutline that they feel sums up the message of the Beatitudes in a snappy way.

Feed back your slogans. You might like to vote on the best one and write it in the oval on the flipchart used in the previous exercise. Be sensitive to group members' feelings and encourage the discussion of several answers before agreeing a key word or phrase as a group.

# >>Get real! (5–10 minutes)

Part of the aim of the course is to help group members to live out the Beatitudes in practical ways.

The following are suggestions of things the group might like to do in the time before the next session. You might want to put these suggestions to the group and then agree a shared activity or common focus, or you might prefer to give group members the freedom to pursue an individual project or course of action. You and your group may have suggestions of your own, in which case go with your own ideas.

> - Learn the Beatitudes by heart, in whatever version you prefer. Or write your own paraphrase.
> - Make your own response to the Beatitudes in a piece of art or craft work (e.g., a poem).
> - Find examples from the Bible of Jesus or any person living out the Beatitudes.
> - Pick the Beatitude that challenges you the most. During the week, collect examples from your own experience, the arts (e.g. a painting, photograph or fictional character), the media (e.g. news headlines, soap storylines, advertising), which demonstrate either:

  1 The Beatitude being lived out;

  2 The opposite of this Beatitude being lived out.

Encourage the group to bring newspaper cuttings, pictures or things they have made to next week's session.

## >>Go deep . . . (10–15 minutes)

Create a still atmosphere. Again, you could light a candle or play some music.

> > **Encourage** group members to sit in a relaxed posture. They might like to hold their palms upwards in their lap as a sign that they are open to all that God is saying to them.

> > **Explain** that the group will hear a reading by two voices. The first voice will read a set of 'opposite' Beatitudes, written by J. B. Phillips, that highlight the countercultural nature of Jesus' sayings.

> The second voice will read the Beatitudes as they appear in *The Message*, a contemporary-language rendering of the Bible by Eugene H. Peterson. *Make sure you have organized this beforehand so that the readers have time to practise.*

**Reader 1:** Happy are the 'pushers': for they get on in the world.

**Reader 2:** But Jesus said: *You're blessed when you're at the end of your rope. With less of you there is more of God and his rule.*

**Reader 1:** Happy are the hard-boiled: for they never let life hurt them.

**Reader 2:** But Jesus said: *You're blessed when you feel you've lost what is most dear to you. Only then can you be embraced by the One most dear to you.*

**Reader 1:** Happy are they who complain: for they get their own way in the end.

**Reader 2:** But Jesus said: *You're blessed when you're content with just who you are – no more, no less. That's the moment you find yourselves proud owners of everything that can't be bought.*

**Reader 1:** Happy are the blasé: for they never worry over their sins.

**Reader 2:** But Jesus said: *You're blessed when you've worked up a good appetite for God. He's food and drink in the best meal you'll ever eat.*

**Reader 1:** Happy are the slave-drivers: for they get results.

**Reader 2:** But Jesus said: *You're blessed when you care. At the moment of being 'care-ful', you find yourselves cared for.*

**Reader 1:** Happy are the knowledgeable men [people] pf the world: for they know their way around.

**Reader 2:** But Jesus said: You're blessed when you get your inside world – your mind and heart – put right. Then you can see God in the outside world.

**Reader 1:** Happy are the troublemakers: for they make people take notice of them.

**Reader 2:** But Jesus said: You're blessed when you can show people how to cooperate instead of compete and fight. That's when you discover who you really are, and your place in God's family.

**Reader 1:** Happy are the apathetic and the morally compromised: they have no principles to cause offence.

**Reader 2:** But Jesus said: You're blessed when your commitment to God provokes persecution. The persecution drives you even deeper into God's kingdom.

> **Follow** the reading with a time of silent reflection.

# Pray

Use one or more of the following prayers or lead the group in a prayer of your own.

Lord God
we thank you for the values of your upside-down kingdom.
And we thank you that you sent Jesus to show us how
to live them out.
Lord, when we are faint-hearted in following you, strengthen us.
Give us the courage to follow you into hard and dark places
Knowing that you will lead us out the other side
And call us 'Blessed'.
Through Jesus Christ our Lord. Amen.

Creator God
Revealed to us in Christ Jesus
**Make us open to you.**
Holy God
King of Kings and consuming fire
**Make us hungry for justice.**
Loving God
Strong tower and God of all comfort
**Purify our hearts.**
Transforming God
Who shapes us as a potter fashions clay
**Change us into your likeness. Amen.**

Almighty God,
in Christ you make all things new:
transform the poverty of our nature
   by the riches of your grace,
and in the renewal of our lives
make known your heavenly glory;
through Jesus Christ your Son our Lord,
who is alive and reigns with you,
in the unity of the Holy Spirit,
one God, now and for ever.

*Collect for the Second Sunday of Epiphany,* Common Worship

## A Lent Prayer

We come to you in brokenness to find healing
In weakness to find courage
In penitence to find a new beginning
In uncertainty to find a next step
In loneliness to find companionship
In longing to find our life's work
In Lent to find Easter
In the name and strength of Christ. Amen.

*Lynne Chitty*

# >> 2 Living Openly / Beforehand

## Matthew 5.3-4

### >>Aim

In this session we will look at the first two of the Beatitudes ('Blessed are the poor in spirit . . .' and 'Blessed are those who mourn . . .') and consider what it means to live in an open way – open to God, to others, and to the joy and pain around us.

### What you will need

> flipchart and marker pens;

> A4 paper and pens;

> copies of this book (preferably one each);

> candle, objects or images of Christ (if used);

> large pebbles (optional – the sort of thing garden centres sell as 'cobbles' would be suitable);

> for the *Go deep* . . . section: picture images/song lyrics/video or DVD as required.

## >>Background

See the 'Be prepared' section in *Tips for leaders* for thoughts about how to use this material.

> 1   *'Blessed are the poor in spirit,*
>     *for theirs is the kingdom of heaven.'*
>     *(Matthew 5.3)*

# Diamond truth

Being poor in spirit means:

> being open to God, rather than playing God in our lives;

> acknowledging our needs;

> being interdependent rather than independent.

# Consequences

We encounter the kingdom of God, now. Acknowledging our poverty opens the door to a greater awareness of, and a willingness to respond to, God's presence around us.

# Cutting across

. . . the need in our culture to be independent, rather than to enjoy and value our interdependence with God, other people and all creation;

. . . a culture of condemnation that says people have only themselves to blame if they are poor;

. . . the need to possess, rather than enjoying life and creation without having to own everything.

# Missing the point

Matthew 5.3 is **not** saying:

> It is holy to be poor. The Bible is not romantic about poverty but sees it as an injustice and an affliction.

> It is holy to put yourself down – this is false humility.

> It is good to grovel. God is angry when we abuse or 'put down' his creatures or creation. Jesus never behaved like a doormat – he stood his ground.

What a way to run a universe, start a new religion, and promote an alternative way of life for planet earth – to suggest that life is found in being poor. Today, of course, the image consultants and spin doctors would never allow it. 'First impressions', they would tell us, are all important. As a lead focus and soundbite this will not do . . . It just won't work. Only it has! It has inspired some of the greatest manifestations of the human spirit, from Francis of Assisi to Mother Teresa. It has shaped whole communities, monastic and missionary, given hope to countless people who have found themselves at the bottom of life's pile, and guidance to some of the most influential people in history.

*Robert Warren,* Living Well, *p.3*

> **2 'Blessed are those who mourn,**
> **for they will be comforted.'**
> **(Matthew 5.4)**

# Diamond truth

Mourning is about:

> > grieving about the pain and injustice in the world and feeling God's pain about how far things are from his purposes;

> > owning the fact that we are part of the problem;

> > refusing to run from pain – whether our own or that of others.

# Consequences

We become more dependent on the work of the Holy Spirit, who is our comforter and strengthens us. In him we find the energy to change things.

# Cutting across

. . . indifference to the sufferings of others;

. . . compassion fatigue in the face of overwhelming human need;

. . . false optimism and the refusal to face painful reality and hard facts.

# Missing the point

Matthew 5.4 is **not** saying:

> Mourning is only to do with bereavement.

> Christians should have a long-faced and judgemental attitude to life.

> Christians should be pessimists – Jesus overflowed with hope and true confidence in God.

---

It is important to note that Jesus said 'Blessed are those who mourn' rather than 'Blessed are those who are bereaved . . .'

We know with greater clarity today how mourning has various stages – of denial, anger, blaming, and integrating. All too easily this mourning is something which we run from. Bereavement happens to us, mourning is a choice. A choice to turn and face the pain and work through it to a better and more whole future.

Jesus is commending and affirming those who have the courage to face and own their pain, to address it, without abandoning the hope which created the 'gap' in the first place.

*Robert Warren*, Living Well, *pp. 19–20*

---

# >> Living Openly / The Session

## >>Welcome (5 minutes)

### Introduction

Welcome the group back and explain that this session will focus on the first two Beatitudes under the umbrella heading of 'Living Openly'.

### Pray

You might like to do the following exercise in preparation for prayer:

> Acknowledge that group members may have arrived at the session rushing and busy, burdened by things that have happened during the day.

> Encourage them to take a stone from a pre-arranged pile and to hold it in their hands.

> Play a piece of music and invite the group to walk, during the music, to a specific place in the room (the centre of the circle in which you are sitting is probably the best place) and to lay down their stone as a symbol that they are putting preoccupations and hassle to one side.

> Invite the group members, having put down their stone, to sit with palms upwards as a sign of their openness.

Now pray, either in your own words, or using the Course Prayer.

#### Course Prayer

Almighty God,
Thank you that you meet us where we are
And beckon us into your kingdom.
As we journey together
May we encounter Christ Jesus,
Be empowered to live like him,
And understand more fully what it means to be blessed. Amen.

## >>Action replay (10 minutes)

Invite group members to share the things they did during the week as a result of the *Get real!* part of the last session. Keep this focused and brief and try to avoid making it a general 'news' time.

## >>Brainstorm (5 minutes)

Ask the group: *What five things do human beings need most?* Do this individually or in pairs or threes. Make lists on scraps of paper and then share ideas quickly.

## >>Encounter (15 minutes)

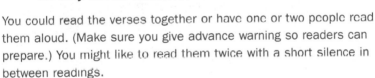

### Read the Beatitudes (Matthew 5.3-4)

> *'Blessed are the poor in spirit,*
> *for theirs is the kingdom of heaven.'*
> *'Blessed are those who mourn,*
> *for they will be comforted.'*

You could read the verses together or have one or two people read them aloud. (Make sure you give advance warning so readers can prepare.) You might like to read them twice with a short silence in between readings.

### Input

Using the *Background* information on pp. 24–7, give a brief talk about this pair of Beatitudes. The following summary may be helpful:

---

The first two Beatitudes are about our attitude to ourselves, life and God. They point to a fundamental openness to God and the whole of life, in all its joys and pains. Celebration and grief are fundamentals of life and of Christian living. Living as creatures before the Creator, we are called to be open to both the richness of all creation and also the brokenness and disorder around us.

---

# >>Talk about it (25 minutes)

We suggest you divide your group into two at this point and
let one group use the material at 1 and the other the material
at 2. (If your group is too small to divide, focus on only one
of the Beatitudes and touch, only briefly, on the second.)

**1** *'Blessed are the poor in spirit, for theirs is the kingdom*
*of heaven.' (Matthew 5.3)*

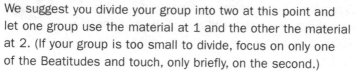

*Be on your guard against all kinds
of greed; a man's life does not consist
in the abundance of his possessions
(Luke 12.15).*

*To be poor in spirit means
that you should never boast about
yourself but see yourself as you are:
useless, no good, stupid.*

*Poor in spirit? Christianity
is just a great big inner putdown.
It's just not good for your self-esteem.
In fact it's masochistic.*

In your group consider some or all of the following questions:

> What do we think it means to be poor in spirit? Write a definition.

> Did Jesus mean it is good to be poor?

> Which of the thought bubbles above do you most identify with?

> Read Jesus' encounter with the rich young ruler (Luke 18.18-25).
  What light does it shed on the first Beatitude?

> Is there any relationship between spiritual and material poverty?
  How does one illuminate the other?

## Jesus focus

*Look at Jesus at his baptism (Matthew 3.13-17).*
How does Jesus help us to define what it means to be poor in spirit?
What *one* word describes Jesus in this incident?

**2** *'Blessed are those who mourn,*
*for they will be comforted.'*
*(Matthew 5.4)*

---

For the Christian, the starting point in . . . mourning is personal
confession and repentance. We dare to face and own our wounds
before attempting to help others, and take the beam out of our own eye
first before helping to remove the speck in the other person's eye. So
mourning is the capacity to face the gap between present reality and
perceived good.

*Robert Warren,* Living Well, *p. 19*

---

In your group consider some or all of the following questions:
> What things do you mourn over?
> Is it helpful to see mourning (as the above quotation
  suggests) as an awareness of the 'gap' between things
  as they are and things as they might be?
> What is the effect on people and communities of refusing
  to mourn? Can you think of examples?
> What is the connection between mourning and repentance?

# Jesus focus

*Read the following passages in which Jesus mourns:*
> Jesus at the grave of Lazarus: John 11.35;
> Jesus weeping over the state of Jerusalem: Matthew 23.37-39;
> Jesus in the garden of Gethsemane: Mark 14.32-42.

What distressed Jesus in each of these situations?
How does that shed light on the second Beatitude?

# Reporting back

If you have been in two groups you might like to report back to each
other at this point. Reporting back can be laboured and boring. To avoid
this, ask someone from each group (possibly a pre-arranged person) to
give one or two headlines of the group's discussion.

If appropriate you could do this in the style of *Just a Minute* where a spokesperson has to say as much as he or she can in one minute. (You could even use a timer!)

## >>Get real! [10 minutes]

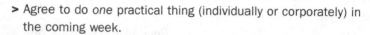

Identify a situation in your family, workplace or local community where demonstrating real 'poverty of spirit' or 'mourning' might make a difference.

> Agree to do *one* practical thing (individually or corporately) in the coming week.

  *OR*

> Watch the news on a daily basis and allow yourself to 'mourn'. Use this as a springboard for practical action and prayer.

## >>Go deep . . . [20 minutes]

Create a still atmosphere. You could light a candle or play some music.

Choose some of the following activities as appropriate to your group:

> **Use picture images** of poverty and mourning. You could collect these from newspapers or magazines or use resources provided by aid agencies such as Oxfam, Christian Aid or Tear Fund. Alternatively you could download images from the internet – go to www.google.co.uk, click on 'Images' and type in the words 'poverty' or 'mourning'. Print images off and mount them on card or photocopy them onto acetates and use on an OHP. If you have the facilities you could use PowerPoint to make a 'slide show'. Show the pictures while playing a piece of music or hand the pictures round the group in silence.

> **Sing, listen to or read aloud** the words of the song 'Kyrie Eleison' (*Let's Praise* 113).

> **Watch** a clip from the film *Phone Booth*.
  We suggest you introduce the extract with the following
  information, run the clip, and then have a brief period of
  silence to reflect on the scene you have watched:

  *New York publicist Stu Sheppard answers a ringing phone in a
  phone booth on a street corner and finds himself talking to a
  sniper with a moral agenda. The sniper, who has a gun trained
  on the phone booth, has been watching Stu and considers
  that he treats other people badly and tells lies. He tells Stu
  that if he puts the phone down he will be shot – that Stu must
  amend his life and learn to tell the truth about himself. For an
  intense 80 minutes Stu is held hostage while the sniper shoots
  a passer-by (making it look like Stu's doing) and threatens to
  shoot either Stu's wife Kelly or his would-be mistress, Pam –
  both of whom have gathered on the pavement with crowds,
  police and TV cameras. Finally at the end of the film, Stu
  breaks down and confesses his sins.*

  **The extract contains strong language and lasts 3 minutes.**

  If using a VCR start at 1:22:16 (where the sniper's voice
  says: 'I'm offering you the chance to redeem yourself . . .')
  and stop at 1:25:44 (after Stu says 'I didn't do it for you').
  If you are using DVD show the whole of scene 23.


> **Read** Isaiah 61.1-3.

  The Spirit of the Sovereign Lord is upon me
  because the Lord has anointed me
  to preach good news to the poor.
  He has sent me to bind up the broken-hearted,
  to proclaim freedom for the captives
  and release from darkness for the prisoners,
  to proclaim the year of the Lord's favour
  and the day of vengeance of our God,
  to comfort all who mourn,
  and provide for those who grieve in Zion –
  to bestow on them a crown of beauty instead of ashes,
  the oil of gladness instead of mourning,
  and a garment of praise instead of a spirit of despair.

> **Read** an extract from *Silas Marner* by George Eliot.
Introduce it with the following information:

*Silas Marner, a miserly reclusive weaver, cares for nothing but his hoarded sack of gold, until one night the gold is stolen. Then, on New Year's Eve, a tiny golden-haired child – orphaned when her mother dies in the snow – crawls into Silas Marner's cottage and falls asleep by his fire. The arrival of this child, Eppie – whom Silas initially mistakes for his returned sack of gold – transforms the old man's life.*

. . . as the weeks grew to months, the child created fresh and fresh links between his life and the lives from which he had hitherto shrunk continually into narrower isolation. Unlike the gold which needed nothing, and must be worshipped in close-locked solitude – which was hidden away from the daylight, was deaf to the song of birds, and started to no human tones – Eppie was a creature of endless claims and ever-growing desires, seeking and loving sunshine, and living sounds, and living movements; making trial of everything, with trust in new joy, and stirring the human kindness in all eyes that looked on her. The gold had kept his thoughts in an ever-repeated circle, leading to nothing beyond itself; but Eppie was an object compacted of changes and hopes that forced his thoughts onward, and carried them far away from their old eager pacing towards the same blank limit – carried them to the new things that would come with the coming years, when Eppie would have learned to understand how her father Silas cared for her; and made him look for images of that time in the ties and charities that bound together the families of his neighbours. The gold had asked that he should sit weaving longer and longer, deafened and blinded more and more to all things except the monotony of his loom and the repetition of his web; but Eppie called him away from his weaving, and made him think all its pauses a holiday, re-awakening his senses with her fresh life.

George Eliot, Silas Marner, *Chapter 14*

# Pray

Use one or both of the following prayers or pray in your own words.

Help us to find that true strength which comes from sharing
our weaknesses,
The true courage that comes from acknowledging our fears,
The true humility that comes from recognizing our pride,
The true voice that comes from encountering our silence,
The true healing that comes from using our wounds,
The true light that comes from facing our darkness,
The true peace that comes from risking ourselves,
And the true life that comes from embracing your death
Lord Jesus,
Amen.

*Lynne Chitty*

**Hear my cry, O God. Listen to my prayer.**
We weep for the poor,
For those without food, or water, or dignity
**Hear my cry, O God. Listen to my prayer.**
We weep for the orphaned,
The comfortless, the refugee.
**Hear my cry, O God. Listen to my prayer.**
We weep for the abused,
Victims of violence, cruelty and war.
**Hear my cry, O God. Listen to my prayer.**
We weep for waste and greed,
And the squandering of your abundance.
**Hear my cry, O God. Listen to my prayer.**
We weep for those oppressed by materialism,
Driven by the need to own and accumulate.
**Hear my cry, O God. Listen to my prayer.**
We weep for ourselves,
For our shallow lives, our smallness and our reluctance
to be vulnerable.
**Hear my cry, O God. Listen to my prayer. Amen.**

# >> 3 Living Purposefully/Beforehand

## Matthew 5.5-6

### >>Aim

In this session we will look at the second two of the Beatitudes ('Blessed are the meek . . .' and 'Blessed are those who hunger and thirst for righteousness . . .') and consider what it means to live by God's agenda.

### What you will need

> - flipchart and marker pens;
> - A4 paper and pens;
> - copies of this book (preferably one each);
> - candle, objects or images of Christ (if used);
> - for *Go deep* . . . section: song lyrics/video/votive candles as required.

## >>Background

See the 'Be prepared' section in *Tips for leaders* (page 13) for thoughts about how to use this material.

> **1** **'Blessed are the meek,**
> **for they will inherit the earth.'**
> **(Matthew 5.5)**

### Diamond truth

Meekness means:

> - receiving life as a gift from God rather than grasping at it;
> - devoting ourselves to God's agenda and priorities in a focused and self-disciplined way;
> - being prepared to lay aside our status and privilege in order to empower and enrich others.

## Consequences

The meek will 'inherit the earth'. Yielding to God's call and purposes will enable us to enter into all that God has planned for us.

## Cutting across

. . . the competitive, achieving instincts of our culture;
. . . the need to be in control;
. . . the need to assert our own importance by putting others down.

## Missing the point

Matthew 5.5 is **not** saying:

> Christians should be wimps.

> Christians should never disagree with anyone – on the contrary, pursuing Godly agendas will surely bring us into conflict with others.

> Christians should act like 'doormats'. Meekness is about yielding to God's agenda rather than fitting in with everybody else's wishes (Romans 12.2).

---

If meekness does not mean weakness, then just what does it mean? An equestrian use of the word can help here. The term is used in the training of the Lipizzaner stallions from the famous Spanish riding school in Vienna. Before they can be trained to perform some amazingly complicated movements they have to be broken in. The term used is 'meeked'. It means to make them biddable and responsive to the trainer.

*Robert Warren,* Living Well, *p. 48*

---

**2  'Blessed are those who hunger and thirst for righteousness, for they will be filled.' (Matthew 5.6)**

# Diamond truth

Hungering and thirsting for righteousness means:

> > aligning our lives with God's priorities and values;

> > longing passionately for the world to be made whole;

> > acting on behalf of others in gentle care and courageous confrontation of evil and injustice.

# Consequences

Those who hunger and thirst 'will be filled'. We experience deep fulfilment as we seek God's kingdom; we are made for God and nothing less will really satisfy us.

# Cutting across

. . . the lie of materialism – that buying and possessing things will satisfy us;

. . . greed for food, sex, or fame;

. . . our culture's instinct to satisfy the needs of 'Number One'.

# Missing the point

Matthew 5.6 is **not** saying:

> > We should be self-righteous or judgemental of others.

> > Righteousness is the same as piety or respectability.

> > Christians should be preoccupied with laws and dogma or with Church activities.

---

[Fulfilment] . . . is discovered as often as not in prayer and in conversation as (poor in spirit) we listen to others, care about what is missing (mourning), and wait (in meekness) to discern the higher agenda (hunger for righteousness). As we seek to do just that, the promise of God is that we will encounter God's presence in the process and – as the long-term consequence – know the satisfaction which engagement with the purposes of God alone can bring.

*Robert Warren,* Living Well, *p. 71*

---

## >>Welcome (5 minutes)

### Introduction

Welcome the group back and explain that this session will focus
on the second two Beatitudes under the umbrella heading of 'Living
Purposefully'.

### Pray

Pray in your own words or use the Course Prayer.

#### Course Prayer

Almighty God
Thank you that you meet us where we are
And beckon us into your kingdom,
As we journey together
May we encounter Christ Jesus,
Be empowered to live like him,
And understand more fully what it means to be blessed. Amen.

## >>Action replay (10 minutes)

Share the things you did during the week as a result of the
*Get real!* part of the last session.

## >>Brainstorm (5 minutes)

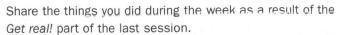

Ask the group: *What gives you satisfaction?*
Do this individually or in pairs or threes. (See p. 17 of the
*Brainstorm* section of Session 1, for suggestions of how to feed
back your answers.)

## >>Encounter (15 minutes)

### Read the Beatitudes (Matthew 5.5-6)

> *'Blessed are the meek, for they will inherit the earth.'*
> *'Blessed are those who hunger and thirst*
> *for righteousness, for they will be filled.'*

You could read the verses together or have one or two people read them aloud. (Make sure you give advance warning so readers can prepare.) You might like to read them twice with a short silence in between readings.

## Input

Using the *Background* information on pp. 36–8 give a brief talk about this pair of Beatitudes. The following summary may be helpful:

---

The second two Beatitudes focus on discovering God's will. Daring to make our lives available to a 'higher agenda', rather than pursuing personal fulfilment, is gloriously demonstrated in Christ as the way to fullness of life. In a culture which understands fulfilment in terms of personal freedom and control, the gospel calls us to live by the truth that God is the one 'whose service is perfect freedom'. Meekness and hunger for righteousness are about availability to God, and his purposes. They will inevitably affect the way we live.

---

## >>Talk about it (30 minutes)

We suggest you divide your group into two at this point and let one group use the material at 1 and the other the material at 2. (If your group is too small to divide, focus on only one of the Beatitudes and touch, only briefly, on the second.)

> **1** *'Blessed are the meek,*
> *for they will inherit the earth.'*
> *(Matthew 5.5)*

'Meekness means committing our lives to fulfil God's plans.'
*Michael Crosby*, Spirituality of the Beatitudes, *p. 113*

In your group consider some or all of the following questions:
> How would you define the quality of 'meekness'?
> Is Jesus encouraging us to be wimps?
> Is meekness the same as being amenable and undemanding?
> How helpful is the image of horses being 'meeked' on p. 37? (See *Background* section of this session.)
> What does it mean to 'inherit the earth'?

## Jesus focus

*Read the account of Jesus washing his disciples' feet at the Last Supper (John 13.3-10).*

What insights does it give into Jesus' own 'meekness'?

> **2 'Blessed are those who hunger and thirst for righteousness, for they will be filled.' (Matthew 5.6)**

The biblical understanding of righteousness fully integrates the personal and the social, the inner and the outer worlds. They become part of one single tapestry, woven together again and again.
*Robert Warren*, Living Well, *p. 67*

In your group consider some or all of the following questions:
> What is the difference between righteousness and self-righteousness?
> What 'righteousness issues' are you most passionate about?
> What are the implications for ourselves and our churches of the above quotation?
> What light does Isaiah 58.6-8 shed on our understanding of 'righteousness'?

## Jesus focus

Jesus was concerned with bringing wholeness to every area of life. He restored Zacchaeus to his community (Luke 18.2-10), enabled the woman with unstoppable bleeding to recover her health (Luke 8.43-48), helped the boy possessed of demons to regain his sanity and dignity (Luke 9.38-42) and restored and reinstated blind, deaf and crippled people marginalized by their disabilities.

*Read Isaiah 42.1-4.*
In what ways does Jesus fulfil Isaiah's description of the 'Suffering Servant'?

## Reporting back

If you have been in two groups you might like to report back to each other at this point. (See the 'Reporting back' section of Session 2 for ideas on how to do this.)

## >>Get real! [10 minutes]

Identify a local or global 'righteousness issue' that you are concerned about as a group. Agree to take some practical action in the coming week. (Be realistic and discuss the nitty-gritty – who is going to do what, and how?)

## >>Go deep . . . [15 minutes]

Create a still atmosphere. You could light a candle or play some music.

Choose some of the following activities as appropriate to your group:

> **Sing, read or listen to** the hymns 'Take my life and let it be' (*Combined Mission Praise* 624) and/or 'Meekness and majesty' (*Combined Mission Praise* 465).

> **Watch** a video of Lipizzaner stallions performing. A 60-minute video, *The Spanish Riding School,* is available from www.longbarntackshop.co.uk at £14.99. There is also the classic film *Miracle of the White Stallions,* which has been released on DVD (2004) and is available to buy from www.amazon.co.uk

> **Read** the 'Christ Hymn' from Philippians 2.4-11.

> **Read** Micah 6.6-8.

# Pray

Use one or more of the following prayers or pray in your own words. (You might like to invite group members to pray silently or aloud for places, people or issues where they 'hunger for righteousness' and to light votive candles.)

O Lord, from whom all good things come:
grant to us your humble servants,
that by your holy inspiration
we may think those things that are good,
and by your merciful guiding may perform the same;
through our Lord Jesus Christ,
who is alive and reigns with you,
in the unity of the Holy Spirit,
one God, now and for ever.

*Collect for Weekdays after Pentecost*

God of the cross,
We offer prayers for all who cry out in pain and despair.
For those who feel forsaken by you and those they love
And for those who, in the last stages of their lives,
   are frightened and alone.
Bless them with the courage that goes beyond fear,
The faith that goes beyond doubt,
The peace that goes beyond terror,
The life that goes beyond death,
And the love that never abandons,
That they may rise with your Son our Saviour Jesus Christ. Amen.

*Lynne Chitty*

From the desert of our materialism
**Good Lord, deliver us.**
From our selfish, privatized culture
**Good Lord, deliver us.**
From our obsession with image and status
**Good Lord, deliver us.**
From our desperate need to control and possess
**Good Lord, deliver us.**
From our compassion fatigue, our apathy and our idleness
**Good Lord, deliver us.**
From a spirituality which fails to embrace humanity
  with all its joys and pains
**Good Lord, deliver us. Amen.**

# >> 4 Living Lovingly/Beforehand

## Matthew 5.7-8

## >>Aim

In this session we look at the third pair of Beatitudes ('Blessed are the merciful . . .' and 'Blessed are the pure in heart . . .') and consider what it means to live in an attitude of love and grace.

### What you will need

> flipchart and marker pens;

> A4 paper and pens;

> copies of this book (preferably one each);

> candle, objects or images of Christ (if used);

> for *Go deep . . .* section: video or DVD, triangles of card and art/collage materials (if doing Seeing God activity).

## >>Background

See the 'Be prepared' section in *Tips for leaders* for thoughts about how to use this material.

> **1** **'Blessed are the merciful,**
> **for they will be shown mercy.'**
> **(Matthew 5.7)**

## Diamond truth

Being merciful means:

> giving to others the same reckless generosity we receive from God;

> being willing to forgive others;

> seeking the best for others, however costly to ourselves, without being either hostile or apathetic to their wrongdoing;

> overcoming evil with good.

## Consequences

'. . . they will receive mercy.'
Demonstrating mercy to others opens us to the mercy of God and others. If we deal in generous portions, we will receive generously (Matthew 7.2).

## Cutting across

. . . the urge to 'get even' with others;
. . . hostility to people who wrong us;
. . . apathy in the face of wrongdoing.

## Missing the point

Matthew 5.7 is **not** saying:

> Wrong things don't matter.

> We should avoid conflict by 'letting people off the hook'.

---

Mercy is . . . about doing good to others and giving them what is needed for their fuller experience of life. Mercy is part of a 'virtuous spiral' or current of grace. As we come to recognize God's goodness and generosity, forgiveness and delight towards us, it becomes the fuel on which our self-worth and self-acceptance run. We are able to give as good as God gives us.

*Robert Warren*, Living Well, *p. 97*

---

**2 'Blessed are the pure in heart,
for they will see God.'
(Matthew 5.8)**

# Diamond truth

Being 'pure in heart' means:

> being sincere in our actions and motives;

> being honest about self and 'real' in relationship to others;

> seeing into the heart of things, beyond the immediate and obvious;

> perceiving God's purposes.

# Consequences

'. . . they will see God.'

For the 'pure in heart' there is the promise of relationship with God.
By rejecting the distorting effects of manipulative behaviour and impure
motives and embracing an honest, trusting attitude, we see beyond the
immediate, to recognize the possible, and God as the source of all our
'possibility thinking'.

# Cutting across

. . . cynicism and the culture of suspicion;

. . . a tendency to see bad in everything and everyone;

. . . a reluctance to trust others.

# Missing the point

Matthew 5.8 is **not** saying:

> Be 'so heavenly minded that we are no earthly use'.

> Be 'too good to be true' or slavishly 'nice'.

> Turn a blind eye to wrong or avoid conflict.

---

Purity of heart does not seem to be about any sort of 'practice'.
It is essentially a private, even hidden work . . . It is about the inner
stillness, waiting and discernment that are at the heart of true justice,
righteousness and the coming of God's kingdom. Purity of heart puts
our own motives, assumptions and expectations in order, so that we
may be part of the solution in the situations around us, rather than
part of the problem itself.

*Robert Warren, Living Well, pp. 106–7*

---

## >>Welcome (5 minutes)

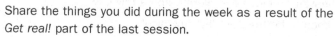

### Introduction

Welcome the group back and explain that this session will focus on the third pair of Beatitudes under the umbrella heading of 'Living Lovingly'.

### Pray

Pray in your own words or use the Course Prayer.

> #### Course Prayer
>
> Almighty God
> Thank you that you meet us where we are
> And beckon us into your kingdom.
> As we journey together
> May we encounter Christ Jesus,
> Be empowered to live like him,
> And understand more fully what it means to be blessed. Amen.

## >>Action replay (10 minutes)

Share the things you did during the week as a result of the *Get real!* part of the last session.

## >>Brainstorm (5 minutes)

Ask the group: *How do you like to be treated?*
Invite individuals to write down or call out words and phrases.
You might like to write them on a flipchart.

# >>Encounter [15 minutes]

## Read the Beatitudes [Matthew 5.7-8]

> *'Blessed are the merciful, for they will receive mercy.'*
> *'Blessed are the pure in heart, for they will see God.'*

You could read the verses together (make sure everyone has a copy they can read) or have one or two people read them aloud. (Make sure you give advance warning so readers can prepare.)

You might like to read them twice with a short silence in between readings.

## Input

Using the *Background* information on pp. 45–7 give a brief talk about this pair of Beatitudes. The following summary may be helpful:

---

The third pair of Beatitudes expresses God's care for the world around us. Mercy and purity are both aspects of righteousness, manifesting a loving engagement with God, ourselves, others and all creation. This outgoing engagement with the whole of life is evident in the abundant life Jesus lived and offered to all.

---

# >>Talk about it [30 minutes]

We suggest you divide your group into two at this point and let one group use the material at 1 and the other the material at 2. (If your group is too small to divide, focus on only one of the Beatitudes and touch, only briefly, on the second.)

> **1** *'Blessed are the merciful,*
> *for they will receive mercy.'*
> *(Matthew 5.7)*

The quality of mercy is not strained,
It droppeth as the gentle rain from heaven
Upon the place beneath. It is twice blest,
It blesseth him that gives and him that takes.

*Portia, in* The Merchant of Venice, *Act IV Scene I*

In your group, consider some or all of the following questions:

> Does showing mercy encourage people to take advantage of you?

> Should governments demonstrate mercy? How?

> How and where have you experienced mercy?

> Is it true in your experience that the measure you use for others is the measure that is used for you?

> What light does the quotation from The Merchant of Venice shed on Jesus' words about mercy?

> Twice, in Matthew 9.13 and Matthew 12.7, Jesus quotes Hosea's observation that God desires 'mercy not sacrifice'. Why is this so important to Jesus?

## Jesus focus

Mercy is active not passive. It reaches out and includes the socially outcast or physically weak, it gives to the needy and challenges the structures of society.

*Look at Jesus in Luke 13.10-17.*
How does he demonstrate mercy?

> **2** **'Blessed are the pure in heart**
> **for they will see God.'**
> **(Matthew 5.8)**

---

Purity of heart clarifies vision

*Simon Tugwell,* Reflections on the Beatitudes, *p. 98*

---

In your group consider some or all of the following questions:

> Is pure the same as 'nice'?

> What is the connection between purity of heart and seeing clearly?

> What difference would an absence of cynicism make in your community?

> Is it naive to see the best and the possible in people and situations?

> Write your own definition of 'purity of heart'.

## Jesus focus

*Look at the account of Jesus' temptation in Matthew 4.1-11.*
Here Jesus' needs, motives and desires are all on trial. In what ways is he 'pure of heart'?

## Reporting back

If you have been in two groups you might like to report back to each other at this point. (See the 'Reporting back' section of Session 2 for ideas on how to do this.)

## >> Get real! [10 minutes]

> Invite group members to think of practical ways they can 'live' mercy and/or purity of heart as individuals in the coming week.

*OR*

> Think of *one* thing your group or the wider church can do to include the marginalized or to challenge unmerciful structures.

## >> Go deep . . . [15 minutes]

Create a still atmosphere. You could light a candle or play some music.

Choose some of the following activities as appropriate to your group:

> **Watch** an extract from the film *The Pianist*. We suggest you introduce the extract with the following information, watch the clip, and then have a brief period of silence to reflect on the scene you have watched:

*Concert pianist Wladyslaw Szpilman, a Polish Jew, has lived through the Second World War, seeing his people stripped of wealth, rights and dignity. His parents, brother and two sisters have all been sent to their deaths in concentration camps and Wladyslaw has witnessed years of shootings, bombings and indescribable brutality. Towards the end of the war – starving and in hiding in the wreckage of occupied Warsaw – Wladyslaw comes face to face with a senior German officer while trying to open a tin of food with a fire poker. Wladyslaw expects the German to kill him but the officer is merciful. Leaving him to continue hiding in the ruined building, the German later returns with a parcel of supplies.*

Either start the video at 2:04:22 (Wladyslaw trying to open the tin of food) and stop at 2:17:30 (where the German officer leaves after giving Wladyslaw his coat) – **a 13-minute clip;**

*OR*

Start the video at 2:14:50 (when the German officer returns to Wladyslaw's hiding place with a parcel) and run to 2:17:30 as above – **a 3-minute clip.**

> **Read** aloud 1 John 2.29–3.3.

> **Seeing God** – a word collage: Give group members a triangle of card or paper each (equilateral triangles work best) in a variety of colours.

Ask each person to write on their triangle one word that describes what God is like.

Now lay the triangles on the floor or on a low table, fitting them together in diamond or hexagon shapes face upwards, so that they look like a cut diamond reflecting many aspects of God.

> **Seeing God** – a picture collage: On a low table in the middle of the room (or on the floor if appropriate) lay out a piece of paper or card (A3 or bigger), some glue sticks, and an assortment of art and collage materials, e.g. oil pastels, coloured wool, sequins, glitter, feathers, coloured foil.

Invite group members, one at a time, to stick something onto the paper or make a mark of some kind to represent one aspect of God. For example, a strip of gold foil to represent God's glory; a feather for God's tenderness; a red pastel zig-zag for God's anger at injustice. You might suggest that they say the quality they are representing out loud as they do it.

Encourage people to be spontaneous and not to worry what the end product looks like or to try to be too literal or figurative.

You could play a piece of music such as a movement from Handel's *Messiah* as a background to this activity.

# Pray

Use one or more of the following prayers or pray in your own words.

> Almighty God,
> to whom all hearts are open,
> all desires known,
> and from whom no secrets are hidden:
> cleanse the thoughts of our hearts
> by the inspiration of your Holy Spirit,
> that we may perfectly love you,
> and worthily magnify your holy name;
> through Jesus Christ our Lord. Amen.
> > *Prayer of Preparation (Collect for Purity),* Common Worship

> For our hostility to those who wrong us
> **Have mercy, O God.**
> For our desire to seek revenge and get even when we are hurt
> **Have mercy, O God.**
> For our apathy to wrongdoing and our unwillingness
>    to face hard truths
> **Have mercy, O God.**

From insincerity, and phoney sentiments
**Purify our hearts.**
From self-delusion and shallow motives
**Purify our hearts.**
From lust and loathing and corrosive cynicism
**Purify our hearts.**

In your glory and majesty
**Lord, may we see you.**
In your holiness and anger
**Lord, may we see you.**
In your mercy and tenderness
**Lord, may we see you. Amen.**


The silence of your love embraces me
I sense a smile,
An arm outstretched
So still we sit,
So still.
Each breath is wonder,
Each thought is joy.
Unmarred by words,
Unspoilt.
O perfect love explode,
Drench us, drown us,
Deafen us to all our self-made noise
To all except
The silence of your love. Amen.

*Lynne Chitty*

# Matthew 5.9-10

## >>Aim

In this session we look at the final pair of Beatitudes ('Blessed are the peacemakers . . .' and 'Blessed are those who are persecuted for righteousness' sake . . .') and consider what it means to live in ways that are radically different and life-affirming.

### What you will need

> flipchart and marker pens;

> copies of this book (preferably one each);

> candle, objects or images of Christ (if used);

> for *Go deep* . . . section: song lyrics as required.

## >>Background

See the 'Be prepared' section in *Tips for leaders* for thoughts about how to use this material.

**1** *'Blessed are the peacemakers
for they will be called children of God.'
(Matthew 5.9)*

## Diamond truth

Being a peacemaker means:

> being constructive not destructive;

> sharing in God's mission to bring wholeness ('Shalom')
to the world;

> facing reality and seeking to resolve conflicts;

> respecting all people, and the earth and its resources.

## Consequences

'. . . they shall be called children of God.' By peacemaking we share in God's nature – when we are making peace we are most like him.

## Cutting across

. . . the need to win battles;

. . . our instinct to avoid conflict;

. . . our urge to be the best and the strongest.

## Missing the point

Matthew 5.9 is **not** saying:

> Try to keep everybody happy all of the time.

> Turn a blind eye to things that are wrong in yourselves, the Church or the world.

> 'Pour oil on troubled waters.'

> Be passive and don't challenge the status quo.

---

The striking promise in this Beatitude is that those who make peace will be called children of God. It underlines just how central to the nature of God peacemaking is. It is how righteousness works out in a fallen world; not in judgement and condemnation but in bringing the fragments together, and building a new picture and experience of harmony.

*Robert Warren*, Living Well, *p. 142*

---

2 **'Blessed are those who are persecuted because of righteousness, for theirs is the kingdom of heaven.' (Matthew 5.10)**

## Diamond truth

Being persecuted for righteousness' sake means:

> > being willing to stand out from the crowd even if this means being thought odd or subversive;

> > speaking and standing up for what is true and right;

> > being prepared to go against the flow.

## Consequences

Being willing to be identified as a Christian and to pursue righteousness mark a person out as 'of the kingdom'. Jesus promises blessings for those who embrace this costly call.

## Cutting across

. . . the pressure to conform;

. . . the need to be liked or popular.

## Missing the point

Matthew 5.10 is **not** saying:

> > We should be deliberately offensive.

> > We should be insensitive or uncaring about the impact of what we say or do.

> > We should look for trouble.

> > We are right and those who oppose us or disagree with us are wrong!

---

The goal is not persecution, but holding on to the will of God. The Beatitudes alert us to the fact that there may well be a real cost in following our vocation, but that problems and trials should neither come as a surprise nor knock us off our guard. We know that, in following Christ, we will be sustained and that any suffering will bear fruit in the long run. For us, as it was for Jesus, trials are the consequence of being fully alive to God and to the world around us.

*Robert Warren,* Living Well, *p. 151*

---

# >> Living Differently / The Session

## >>Welcome (5 minutes)

### Introduction

Welcome the group back and explain that this session will focus on the last two Beatitudes under the umbrella heading of 'Living Differently'.

### Pray

Pray in your own words or use the Course Prayer.

> #### Course Prayer
>
> Almighty God
> Thank you that you meet us where we are
> And beckon us into your kingdom.
> As we journey together
> May we encounter Christ Jesus,
> Be empowered to live like him,
> And understand more fully what it means to be blessed. Amen.

## >>Action replay (10 minutes)

Share the things you did during the week as a result of the *Get real!* part of the last session.

## >>Brainstorm (5 minutes)

Ask the group: *What is peace?*
Invite individuals to write down or call out words and phrases.
You might like to write them on a flipchart.

## >>Encounter (15 minutes)

### Read the Beatitudes (Matthew 5.9-10)

> *'Blessed are the peacemakers*
> *for they will be called children of God.'*
> *'Blessed are those who are persecuted*
> *for righteousness' sake, for theirs is the*
> *kingdom of heaven.'*

You could read the verses together (make sure everyone has a copy they can read) or have one or two people read them aloud. (Make sure you give advance warning so readers can prepare.)

You might like to read them twice with a short silence in between readings.

## Input

Using the *Background* information on pp. 55–7 give a brief talk about this pair of Beatitudes. The following summary may be helpful:

---

The final two Beatitudes are about sharing in God's mission in the world today. Overcoming evil with good is a key principle in the whole ministry of Jesus. It took him as far as the Cross. It is a characteristic pointed to by Paul (Romans 12.21) and described in Revelation as the heart of what it is to be a believer – *an overcomer*. Peacemaking will get us into trouble (persecution) from all sides.

---

## >>Talk about it (25 minutes)

We suggest you divide your group into two at this point and let one group use the material at 1 and the other the material at 2. (If your group is too small to divide, focus on only one of the Beatitudes and touch, only briefly, on the second.)

> 1  *'Blessed are the peacemakers*
> *for they will be called children of God.'*
> *(Matthew 5.9)*

To share today in Christ's peacemaking work involves us in the same range of activities; caring about people's bodies and physical well-being, addressing underlying negative and hostile attitudes that block wholeness and justice, engaging in radical actions of counting others in rather than keeping them out, and being prepared for the deep conflicts that are required if we are to 'give peace a chance'.

*Robert Warren*, Living Well, *p. 138*

In your group, consider some or all of the following questions:

> How should Christians resolve conflict?

> Is being a peacemaker the same as being passive or easy-going?

> How and where could you 'make peace'?

> Why is peacemaking so important to God?

> Are peacemakers always pacifists?

> What is the connection between making peace and pursuing social justice?

## Jesus focus

*Look at Jesus 'cleansing the temple' in Matthew 21.10-16.*
Is Jesus a peacemaker in this incident?

**2 'Blessed are those who are persecuted for righteousness' sake, for theirs is the kingdom of heaven.'
(Matthew 5.10)**

Persecution is an embarrassment to Western Christians; or rather, the lack of it is. There is so much in the scriptures that prepares the disciple for a rough ride, for suffering and pain, in this world that when it does not happen we are thrown by the experience. Are we simply not worth persecuting, we wonder?

*Robert Warren*, Living Well, *p. 147*

In your group, consider some or all of the following questions:

> In the light of the above quote, are we worth persecuting?

> How do we discern when hostility is 'persecution' and when it is deserved censure?

> What persecution have you suffered?

> What *one* thing might God be calling you to do that goes 'against the flow'?

> How can we respond to the sufferings of persecuted Christians elsewhere in the world?

## Jesus focus

*Read Isaiah 53.3,7.*
How does this description of the 'Suffering Servant' anticipate Jesus' suffering on the cross?

## >>Get real! (5 minutes)

> **Watch the news** on a daily basis and use it to pray for peace in national and global trouble spots.

OR

> **Identify an issue** – local or global – where your group could actively work for peace and decide on *one* practical thing you could do to make a difference.

## >>Go deep . . . (25 minutes)

As this is the last session, use this final time of reflection to look back on the course as a whole and to consider how you will try to live out the Beatitudes in the future. You could do this in a number of ways:

> Ask each group member to share one thing they feel they have learned, grasped or re-grasped during the course. (You could prepare them in advance for this by mentioning this exercise at the end of the previous session.)

> Ask each group member the Beatitude which has most changed them and affected them during the course.

> Ask each group member to read or recall the quote, extract or image that has made most impact on them in the previous four sessions. (Again, prepare group members for this by giving prior warning.)

> Invite group members to bring along or share something they have made, found or noticed during the weeks of the course. (See the suggestions for creative activities in the *Get real!* section of Session 1. Again, give the group advance warning so they can prepare.)

Having shared ideas, insights and responses together in the group, you could do one or more of the following activities:

> **Create a still atmosphere** by lighting a candle or playing some music.

> **Sing, read aloud or listen** to the song 'Will you come and follow me?' (*Common Ground* 148).

> **Read** the Beatitudes (Matthew 5.3-10) aloud as a whole.

# Pray

Pray in your own words or using one or more of the following prayers:

### Disturb me O Lord,

Disturb me until I cannot stand, until I cannot think,
   until I cannot pray.
Disturb me until I am still enough to rest in your presence.
Then send me out in your service to disturb others in Christ's
   name. Amen.

*Lynne Chitty*

Almighty God,
by whose grace alone we are accepted
   and called to your service:
strengthen us by your Holy Spirit
and make us worthy of our calling;
through Jesus Christ your Son our Lord,
who is alive and reigns with you,
in the unity of the Holy Spirit,
one God, now and for ever.
            *Collect for the Fifth Sunday before Lent,* Common Worship


Reveal, O Lord, to my eyes your glory.
Expose, O Lord, to my heart your love.
Disperse, O Lord, from my mind the darkness.
Fill, O Lord, my mind with your light.
Protect, O Lord, from thoughts without action.
Guard, O Lord, from words without feelings.
Defend, O Lord, from ideas without results.
And surround me with your presence.
Upon my eyes
My heart
My mind
My will
My soul
To the blowing of your Spirit.
            *David Adam,* Tides and Seasons, *p. 43*



May the love of the Lord Jesus
Draw us to himself;
May the power of the Lord Jesus
Strengthen us in his service;
May the joy of the Lord Jesus
Fill our souls.
May the blessing of God almighty,
The Father, the Son, and the Holy Ghost,
Be amongst you
And remain with you always.
            *William Temple*

# >> Bibliography
## and further Resources

David Adam, *Tides and Seasons*, SPCK, 2010.

Michael Crosby, *Spirituality of the Beatitudes* (revised edition), Orbis Books, 2005.

Stephen Cottrell, *Hit the Ground Kneeling: Seeing leadership differently*, Church House Publishing, 2008.

Steven Croft, *Jesus' People*, Church House Publishing, 2009.

S. Cottrell, S. Croft, J. Finney, F. Lawson and R. Warren, *Emmaus: Leading an Emmaus Group* (second edition), Church House Publishing, 2004.

George Eliot, *Silas Marner*, Penguin, 2003.

Peter Horrobin and Greg Leavers (eds), *Complete Mission Praise*, Collins, 2010

Henri Nouwen, *Bread for the Journey: Reflections for Every Day of the Year*, Darton, Longman & Todd, 1997.

Eugene H. Peterson, *The Message: Remix*, NavPress, 2004.

Simon Tugwell, *Reflections on the Beatitudes: Soundings in Christian Traditions*, Darton, Longman & Todd, 1980.

Robert Warren, *Living Well*, HarperCollins, 1998.

Walter Wink, *Transforming Bible Study*, Wipf & Stock, 2009.

Philip Yancey, *The Jesus I Never Knew*, Zondervan, 2002.

# filmography

Arthur Hiller (director), *Miracle of the White Stallions*, Disney, 1963.

Roman Polanski (director), *The Pianist*, Universal Pictures, 2003.

Joel Schumacher (director), *Phone Booth*, Twentieth Century Fox, 2003.

*The Spanish Riding School: The First 400 Years*, 1987.

CPSIA information can be obtained
at www.ICGtesting.com
Printed in the USA
FSOW03n1324130116
15551FS

9 780715 142332